THE STORY OF
KING JESUS

BEN IRWIN
ILLUSTRATED BY NICK LEE

David C Cook
transforming lives together

THE STORY OF KING JESUS
Published by David C Cook
4050 Lee Vance View
Colorado Springs, CO 80918 U.S.A.

David C Cook Distribution Canada
55 Woodslee Avenue, Paris, Ontario, Canada N3L 3E5

David C Cook U.K., Kingsway Communications
Eastbourne, East Sussex BN23 6NT, England

All Scripture quotations are taken from the Holy Bible, New International
Version®, NIV®. Copyright © 1973, 2011 by Biblica, Inc.™ Used by permission
of Zondervan. All rights reserved worldwide. www.zondervan.com.

LCCN 2014948793
ISBN 978-1-4347-0772-7
eISBN 978-0-7814-1281-0

© 2015 Ben Irwin

The Team: Catherine DeVries, Ingrid Beck, Elisa Stanford, Helen Macdonald, Karen Athen
Cover Design and Illustration: Nick Lee

Printed in Shenzhen, Guangdong Province, China, in October 2014 by Imago.
First Edition 2015

1 2 3 4 5 6 7 8 9 10

For my daughter, Elizabeth—you inspired this book.
For my son, Oliver, and my godson, Joseph.
May you come to embrace this story as your own.
—Ben

For Ruby and Jonas.
—Nick

It all began with God.

God made everything you can see.
(And even things you can't see!)

God made the world to be his home.

Then God made the very first people so he could share his home with them. God gave them a beautiful garden to live in. He gave them a job to do: take care of his good world and help him rule over it.

But they didn't listen to God.

The very first people didn't like doing things God's way. They wanted to do things their own way. They wanted to be in charge.

So they took what wasn't theirs. They tried to rule the world for themselves.

And so the very first people had to leave the garden that God had made for them.

After this, everyone tried to do things their own way, from the very first people all the way to you and me.

God's good world was broken.

But God never stopped loving his people. He promised to make the world right and good again so we could live with him and he could be our King.

God had a plan, and it started with Abraham.

God gave Abraham children and grandchildren and great-grandchildren.

Abraham's family became a great nation. God named them "Israel."

God made Israel his chosen people. They would help him make the world right and good again.

God went with Israel everywhere they went. When they were slaves in another country, God was with them. When they were treated badly, God rescued them.

God gave Israel a home. He gave them laws to follow so they would know how to show their love for him and for each other. God also gave them a very important job: to show the world what it means to be God's people.

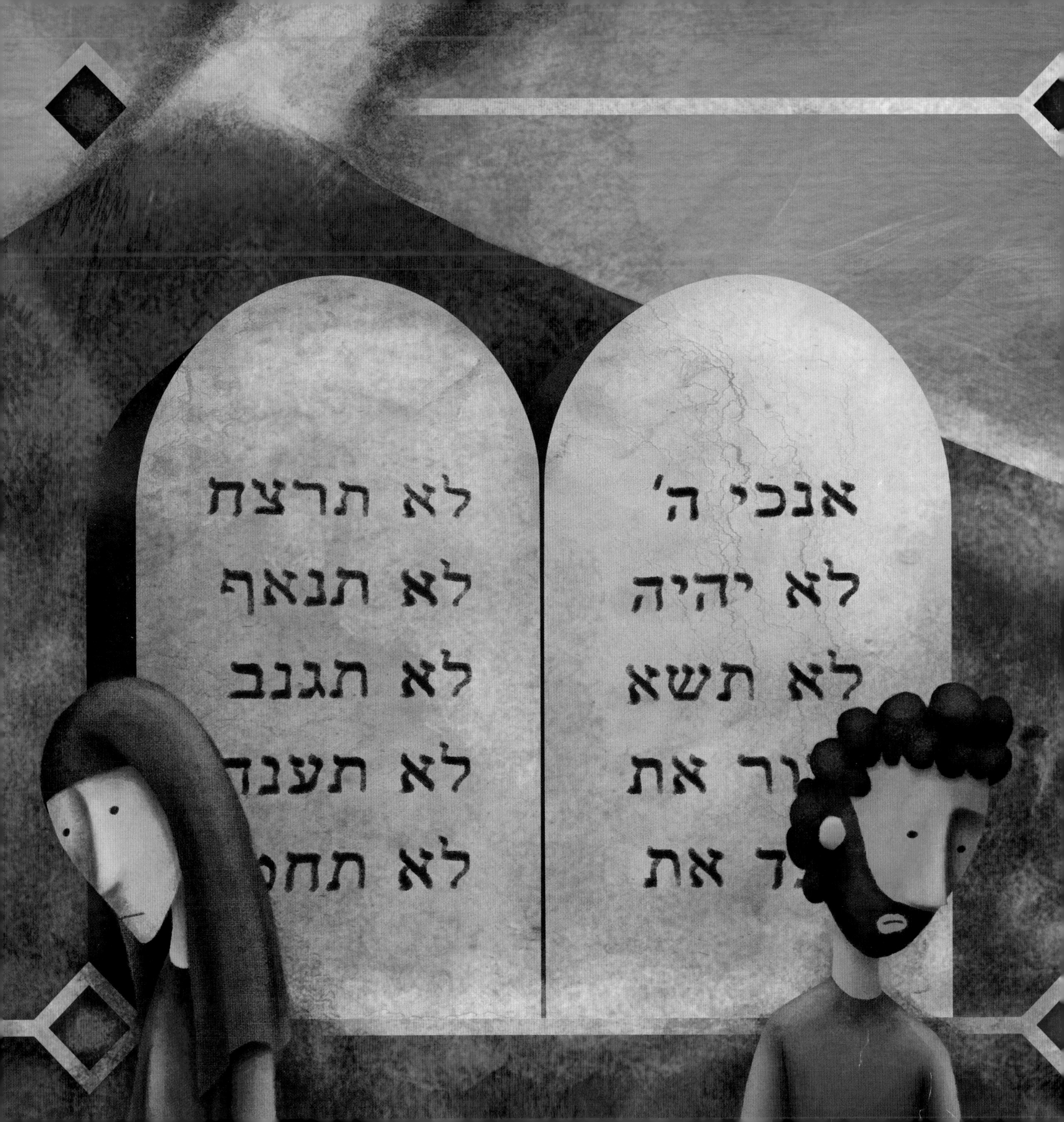

אנכי ה׳
לא יהיה
לא תשא
את
את
לא תרצח
לא תנאף
לא תגנב
לא
לא

God told Israel, "If you let me be your King, you will have a good life. I will live with you, and you will help me make the world right and good again."

But Israel didn't listen.

God's people were just like the very first people. They didn't want God telling them how to live. They wanted to do things their own way.

God's people didn't want God to be their King. Instead, they wanted their king to be a person just like them.

So he let Israel have a king. Then another king. And another.

Some kings were good. Some were bad.

Mostly, the kings did whatever they wanted. They didn't want God to be in charge. So they took what wasn't theirs. They ruled Israel for themselves and not for God.

They did things their own way.

So God sent prophets to remind the kings and their people that there was only one true King. There was only one true God.

But the kings and the people wouldn't listen. So they had to leave their home. Other nations came and conquered Israel. They carried God's people away.

Years went by. People didn't hear
from God like they used to.
Instead, they heard only … silence.

Until …

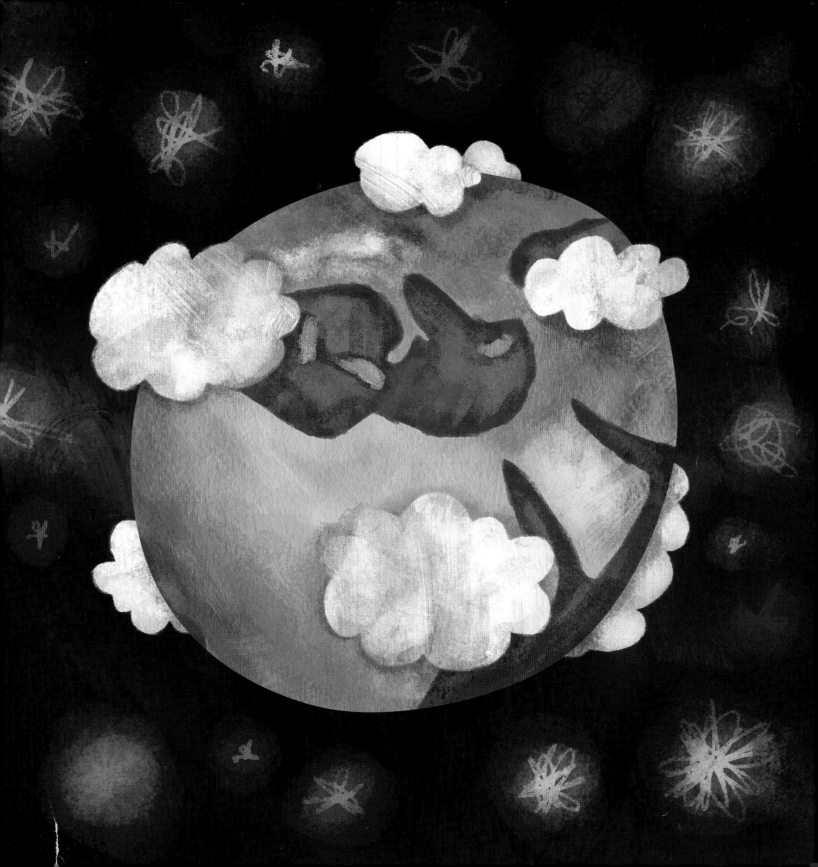

Something new happened. God had a plan. He sent Someone special.

God sent Someone who would rule the world as King. But this Person wouldn't rule like the kings of Israel. This Person would rule the way God wanted.

God sent his only Son, Jesus,
his Chosen One, to rescue Israel and
make the world right and good again.

Because God still had a plan.

When Jesus grew up, he did good things everywhere he went. He healed the sick. He fed the hungry. He rescued people from all sorts of problems.

Jesus did everything God wanted.

But some people still didn't want to do things God's way. They didn't want Jesus to be their King. They still wanted to be in charge of themselves.

So one day, some powerful people decided to stop Jesus before he could take away their power.

They arrested Jesus. They took off his clothes.
They nailed him to a wooden cross
and watched him die.

Jesus never fought back. He never raised a sword.
He never even raised a finger.

The powerful people thought they had won. They thought they had beaten God's Chosen One. They thought they had stopped Jesus from becoming King.

But there was something they didn't understand:
Jesus didn't have to die.

Jesus chose to die for the powerful people and for
the very first people and for all of us too.
Jesus, the one true King, died in our place.
He died to make the world right and good again.

But no one understood.

Then God did something wonderful.

The same God who made the world, rescued Israel, and sent Jesus—he did the most wonderful, surprising thing of all.

God raised Jesus from the dead.

But Jesus didn't just rise from the dead; he defeated death
so it wouldn't have power over us any longer. Jesus made it
possible for us to be God's people again. He made it possible
for us to live the way God wants.

God gave us the King we needed. God gave us Jesus, a King who loves, forgives, and changes everyone who comes to him.

Our King gave us a job to do:
love each other with all we've got.
That's how we show God's love to
everyone else.

For now, the world is still broken. We still take what isn't ours. We don't always love each other the way God wants us to.

But someday, Jesus our King is coming back. He will make the world right and good again. He will make the world his home again, and it will be a place where we love each other the way God loves us.

God will live with us. We will help him rule the world, and he will be our King.

Forever.

NOTE TO PARENTS

In the Bible, when the Israelites wanted to pass their faith to the next generation, they shared their ancient story of rescue: "We were slaves of Pharaoh in Egypt, but the LORD brought us out of Egypt with a mighty hand" (Deuteronomy 6:21). Stories have the power to nurture children's curiosity and to engage their imaginations.

Telling the story of redemption—how God became King, how he's making the world right again so he can dwell with us—has the power to transform a child's life. That's what this book is about.

God's redemptive tale can't be reduced to a few memory verses from Scripture. It's not a formula or a plan or a prayer you recite. It's a drama that you live, and it's woven throughout every book of the Bible, from Genesis to Revelation.

The story presented in this book is short enough that you can read it in one sitting, yet long enough that you and your children can come back to it again and again. Encourage your children to ask questions as you read. Talk about the details in the pictures. Use this book as a launching point to explore the Bible together.

Most of all, show your children—with your life and words—that this is your story, and it can be theirs too.

Ben Irwin